MANZ-LERNHILFEN

Hannes Gumtau
Wolfgang Kurschatke

Realschulabschluß Englisch

Reading Comprehension Tests
Prüfungsaufgaben 3

(1979–1983)

manz

MANZ VERLAG MÜNCHEN

Herausgegeben von Ute Kretschmann

Manzbuch 580

6 5 1985 84 83
(Die jeweils letzte Zahl bezeichnet die Auflage bzw. das Erscheinungsjahr)

Gesamtherstellung: Verlag und Druckerei G.J. Manz AG, München/Dillingen
Printed in Germany

ISBN 3-7863-0580-3

Inhalt

A) Schwerpunkte der Abschlußprüfungen:

B) Lernhilfen für den Schüler:

C) Aufgaben der Abschlußprüfungen in Bayern:

A) Schwerpunkte der Abschlußprüfungen.

Wortschatz

	1983A	1983B	1982A	1982B	1981A	1981B	1980A	1980B	1979A	1979B
1. Synonyms Wörter mit ähnlicher Bedeutung.	4–9	7–10	9–11	9–11	10–13	5–8	6–9	8–10	6–8	11–15
2. Explanations Definitions Erklärung von Wörtern oder Ausdrücken.										
a) multiple choice Auswahl-Antwort	1–3	1–2	1–4	1, 4	1–3		1–3	1–3	1–4	1–3
b) Lückentext							10–11	11–12	5	
c) selbständige Erklärungen	10–12	5–6	12, 13						11–13	4–6
3. Opposites Wörter mit entgegengesetzter Bedeutung.					14–16		4–5	6–7		7–10
4. Word Families Wörter aus der gleichen Wortfamilie.			5–8	7, 8	7–9	9–12				
5. Words from the text / from a list		3–4		5, 6	4–6	1–4				

Fragen zum Text

	1983A	1983B	1982A	1982B	1981A	1981B	1980A	1980B	1979A	1979B
6. Questions on the text Fragen, die sich auf den Text beziehen.	13–17	11–15	14–16	2, 3 12–14	17–20	13–17	12–16	13–15	14–17	16–19
7. Additional (= Further) Questions **a) Weiterführende Fragen zum Text**	18			15, 16	21–22	18	17	16	18–21	20
b) Persönliche Stellungnahmen	19	16–17	17, 18	17, 18	23	19–20	18	17–18		21
8. Defective Dialogue Bildung von Fragen zu vorgegebenen Antworten.	25–27						19–22	19–22		22–27
9. True or false Begründung einer Aussage.										
10. Guided Writing Bildung von Sätzen aus vorgegebenen Teilen.			19–21	26	24–25	21–22			39	

Grammatik

	1983A	1983B	1982A	1982B	1981A	1981B	1980A	1980B	1979A	1979B
11. Tenses Gebrauch der Zeiten (Kontext; Signalwörter).	20–24	18–36 37–38	27, 28, 29, 31, 32, 34	19–25	26 36–40		23	26	31	28–35
12. Passive Gebrauch des Passivs oder Umformung.	20 23	18, 20	30, 31, 34	22, 24	27, 29 35–37		24	26	32–33	
13. If-Clauses Zeitenfolge in Konditionalsätzen	21		33	19, 20	28		26		25	
14. Reported Speech Umformung von der direkten in die indirekte Rede, oder umgekehrt.		39–41				26–29		23–25	27–29	
15. Participal Constructions Umformungen von / in Partizipialkonstruktionen.					31–32	30–33	30		36–38	36–40

	1983A	1983B	1982A	1982B	1981A	1981B	1980A	1980B	1979A	1979B
16. Gerund Gerund nach gewissen Verben oder Präpositionen	21	23	27, 28, 29	24	30		25, 27	26	30	
17. Adjective Adverb Adjektiv oder Adverb? Steigerung	28–30	26–27 32, 34 35	24, 25 26	22	33–34		28		34–35	
18. Relatives Relativ-pronomen Relativ-sätze							28, 32	26	26	36–38
19. Reflexive / Reciprocal Pronouns Einsetzübungen mit Pronomen, falls erforderlich.						23–25			22–24	

Übersetzung ins Deutsche

	1983A	1983B	1982A	1982B	1981A	1981B	1980A	1980B	1979A	1979B
20. Translation										
a) Textabschnitte			35		41				40	41
b) zusätzliche Textstellen	31	42		27		34	33	27		

Die Ziffern, die den Fragen in den jeweiligen Prüfungsarbeiten entsprechen, zeigen die Schwerpunkte der Aufgaben. Sie ermöglichen es, bei der Vorbereitung Akzente zu setzen und einzelne Themen durch verschiedene Abschlußprüfungen zu verfolgen.

B) Lernhilfen für den Schüler:

Allgemeine Tips zur Bearbeitung eines Comprehension Tests

a) Lesen Sie den Text mehrmals gründlich durch.
Unterstreichen Sie einzelne schwierige Wörter und Satzteile. Es ist nicht unbedingt erforderlich, **jedes einzelne** Wort schon zu Beginn der Arbeit zu kennen.

b) Bearbeiten Sie die Aufgaben möglichst der Reihe nach und nehmen Sie immer wieder den Text zu Hilfe.

c) Die Arbeitszeit beträgt 90 Minuten. Benötigen Sie zu viel Zeit für eine Lösung, dann gehen Sie vorläufig zur nächsten Aufgabe über. Beachten Sie auch, wieviele Punkte die Aufgaben wert sind. Bei hoher Punktzahl sind ausführliche Antworten notwendig!
Die Übersetzung ist meist als letzter Teil der Textaufgabe zu bearbeiten und erbringt 25–30% der Gesamtpunktzahl. Beachten Sie dies bei Ihrer Zeitplanung!

d) Versuchen Sie am Schluß, unvollständige und ausgelassene Übungen zu bearbeiten.

e) Gehen Sie die gesamte Prüfung Aufgabe um Aufgabe durch, damit Sie nichts vergessen.
Entscheiden Sie sich für **eine** Lösung, wenn nichts anderes angegeben ist.
Kontrollieren Sie, wo ganze Sätze (»complete sentences«), nur Wörter (»Fill in the words«; Write down the words only«.) bzw. nur Buchstaben (»Write down the number and letter«!) verlangt werden.
Beachten Sie, daß manche Antworten aus mehreren Teilen bestehen (»Name **two** things.« »Give **two** reasons.« »Write **three** sentences.« »Give **three** items.«).

Hilfen für die Aufgaben zum Wortschatz

zu 1. Synonyms

Typische Aufgaben:
Find a **synonym** for each of the following words.
Rewrite the following sentences using **expressions of similar meaning** to the underlined words.
Replace the underlined words or phrases **without changing the meaning** of the sentences.

Lernhilfen:

a) Die Wortart des vorgegebenen und des Lösungswortes muß übereinstimmen.
z.B. Water becomes **scarce.** → Water becomes **rare.** (Adjektiv!)
He runs **quickly.** → He runs **fast.** (Adverb!)
He **receives** money. → He **gets** money. (Verb!)

b) Die Zeitstufe und Form muß bei Verben übereinstimmen.
z.B. He **receives** money. → He **gets** money. (Present!)
He **received** money. → He **got** money. (Past!)
journey**ing** → travell**ing** (ing-Form!)

c) Singular bzw. Plural muß sich bei Substantiven entsprechen.
z.B. Their **route** was blocked. → Their **way** was blocked. (Singular!)
They were rival**s**. → They were opponent**s**. (Plural!)

zu 2. Explanations / Definitions

Typische Aufgaben:
Which is the best **explanation?**
Complete the sentences.
Read the following explanations and write down the letter and number of the best **definition** in each case.
Define the following words.
Use each of the words in a sentence to show the **meaning.**
Explain in a sentence the meaning of the following words or expressions.
Paraphrase the following words.

Lernhilfen:

a) Bei Lückentexten muß das Lösungswort in seiner Form (Zeitstufe; Singular oder Plural) passen.

z. B. Voluntary helpers are people who help **voluntarily**. (Adverb!)
If a person is deaf he or she **can't hear**. (Present!)

b) Für selbständige Erklärungen möchten wir einige Hilfen anführen. Man kann eine knappe Definition ausweiten, indem man denkt . . .

. . . an eine nähere Bestimmung zu Ort oder Lage:
Denmark is a small country **in Northern Europe**.

. . . an genauere Angaben zur Zeit:
Breakfast is the **first** meal **in the morning**.

. . . an Aussagen zum Aussehen oder zu typischen Eigenschaften:
A donkey is an animal **with long ears**.
An onion is a round vegetable **with a strong smell and taste**.

. . . an Tätigkeiten oder Verwendungsmöglichkeiten:
An actor is someone **who plays a part in a film or a play**.
A garage is a place **where cars are kept or repaired**.

c) Definitionen beginnen häufig mit . . .

. . . is someone (oder: a person / a man / a woman / a girl) who . . . **(who bei Personen!)**

. . . is something (oder: a thing / an instrument) which . . . **(which bei Dingen!)**

zu 3. Opposites

Typische Aufgaben:

Finish the following sentences using the **opposites** of the words underlined.
Complete the following sentence using the **opposites** of the underlined words.

Lernhilfen:

a) Die Wortart des vorgegebenen und des zu findenden Wortes muß übereinstimmen.

z. B. It is **quick**. → It is **slow**. (Adjektiv!)
He runs **quickly**. → He runs **slowly**. (Adverb!)

b) Die Zeitstufe und die Form muß bei Verben übereinstimmen.

z. B. He **pushes**. → He **pulls**. (Present!)
He **pushed**. → He **pulled**. (Past!)
push**ing**. → pull**ing** (-ing-Form!)

c) Die Form des Substantivs muß sich entsprechen.

z. B. He is my **enemy**. → He is my **friend**. (Singular!)
They are **enemies**. → They are **friends**. (Plural!)

zu 4. Word families

Typische Aufgaben:

Complete the following sentences. Use **words of the same family** as the ones in brackets.
Find the **corresponding verbs** (oder: **nouns**; oder: **adjectives**).

Lernhilfen:

Denken Sie bitte an folgende Nachsilben, wenn Ihnen das entsprechende Lösungswort nicht gleich einfällt:

a) Substantive bildet man oft mit **-er/-or; -tion/-ation; -ity; -ment; -ness; -ence/-ance; -al; -t; -th.**

z. B. to begin → a beginner; to act → an actor;
to dictate → a dictation; to imagine → an imagination;
active → activity; to develop → the development;
happy → happiness; to differ → the difference;
to appear → the appearance; to arrive → the arrival;
to weigh → the weight; to grow → the growth.

b) Verben bildet man manchmal mit **-en** bzw. **-ize**.

z. B. tight → to tighten; strong → to strengthen;
modern → to modernize; central → to centralize.

c) Adjektive bildet man häufig mit **-able; -ent/-ant; -ful; -less; -ic**.

z. B. fashion → fashionable; to differ → different;
to please → pleasant; care → careful bzw. careless;
drama → dramatic; patriot → patriotic.

Hilfen für die Beantwortung von Fragen zum Text.

zu 6. Questions on the text.

Fragen zum Text beginnen meist mit »who, what, when, where, why, how«. Antworten Sie in ganzen Sätzen (»Answer in complete sentences«). Befolgen Sie zusätzliche Anweisungen genau (»Two facts«; »Three reasons«; »two items«). Beachten Sie, daß Personen und Zeiten in Frage und Antwort gleich sind. Schreiben Sie keine überflüssigen Stellen aus dem Text ab. Verwenden Sie nur die Stellen, die wirklich in der Frage angesprochen sind. Häufig können Sie einen Teil der Frage für den Beginn Ihrer Antwort verwenden: z. B. »Why did he find . . .?« → »He found . . . because . . .«.

zu 7. Additional Questions (= Further Questions)

Einige dieser Fragen gehen über den Text hinaus und sind von Ihrem allgemeinen Wissensstand her zu beantworten.
Andere sind Entscheidungsfragen mit Ihrer persönlichen Stellungsnahme.
Oft wird hier gefragt: »What do **you** think?« »What would **you** have done?« »Give a reason for **your** opinion.«
Hilfen für die Antwort sind z.B. »I think . . . .« »In my opinion . . . .«
Beachten Sie zusätzliche Angaben, was den Umfang Ihrer Lösung betrifft.

zu 8. Defective Dialogue.

Hier müssen Sie die Fragen zu vorgegebenen Antworten stellen. Beachten Sie v. a. die Wortstellung im Fragesatz:
Where do you come from? (Fragepronomen / Hilfsverb / Subjekt / Verb).
Übrigens: »why« heißt »warum« → »weil« heißt »because«;
»who« heißt »wer« → »wo« heißt »where«.

zu 9. True or false.

Bei dieser Aufgabenstellung sollen Sie mit Hilfe des Textzusammenhanges entscheiden, ob ›true‹ (richtig) oder ›false‹ (falsch) in Frage kommt. Meist wird auch eine Begründung verlangt.
Vorschlag für Lösung: This statement is true (false) because . . . (→ Textstelle).

zu 10. Guided Writing.

Sie müssen hier aus vorgegebenen Teilen Sätze bilden.
Besonders beachten: Wortstellung, Zeiten, Einzahl – Mehrzahl.

Hilfen bei den Aufgaben zur Grammatik.

Typische Aufgabenstellungen:
Fill in the forms of the verbs in brackets.
Fill in the forms of the words in brackets.
Fill in the gaps with the correct forms of the words in brackets.
Rewrite the following sentences without using the participial construction underlined.
Rewrite the following sentences replacing the participial constructions.
Rewrite the following sentences replacing the -ing form by a clause.
Write down the report in indirect speech.
Rewrite the questions in indirect speech.
What did they really say? (Use direct speech)
Say the same thing, using a different construction. (Active / Passive)
Complete the following sentences, using the words in brackets in their correct form.

Lernhilfen:

zu 11. Tenses

Bei diesen Übungen stehen die Grundformen der Verben meist in Klammern (= brackets) und Sie müssen die richtigen Zeitstufen bzw. Formen aus dem Zusammenhang erkennen. Signalwörter sind z. B.:
last year / week / month → Past Tense; **next year / week** → Future;
up to now → Present Perfect.
Beachten Sie die Zeitenfolge, z. B.
After **they had shown** (Past Perfect!) . . ., **they were allowed** . . . (Past Tense!).

zu 12. Passive

Das Problem ›Aktiv / Passiv‹ ist oft in der oben genannten Übung (»Tenses«) versteckt. Manchmal werden Umwandlungen verlangt. Beachten Sie dabei v. a.:
Die Zeitstufen bleiben gleich.
Das Objekt im Aktivsatz wird Subjekt im Passivsatz.
Bei der Umformung ins Aktiv muß oft ein sinnvolles Subjekt gefunden werden (»People«, »they«, »you«).

zu 13. If-Clauses

Der Hauptsatz oder der Nebensatz (mit »if«, oder: »on condition«, »in case«, »provided«, »unless«!) wird meist als Lückensatz vorgegeben. Entscheidend für die Zeitenfolge ist der Sinnzusammenhang. Das Grundmuster (Ausnahme: Wunschsätze!) lautet:
If it rains (Present!), I will stay at home (Future!).
If it rained (Past!), I would stay at home (Conditional!).
If it had rained (Past Perfect!), I would have stayed at home (Past Conditional!).

zu 14. Reported Speech

Beachten Sie bei der Umwandlung von der direkten (= direct) in die indirekte (= »indirect oder: reported«) Rede v. a.:

a) Die Pronomen ändern sich (z. B. »I« → »he«)
b) Bei indirekten **Fragen** brauchen wir die normale Satzstellung: S-P-O. (z. B. He asked why they hadn't come.)
c) Wenn **das einleitende Verb in Past Tense oder Past Perfect** steht, ist die Zeitenverschiebung zu beachten:

Present → Past
Future → Conditional
Past → Past Perfect
Present Perfect → Past Perfect

d) Weitere Veränderungen sind z. B.

this → that
today → that day
yesterday → the day before
now → then
here → there
tomorrow → the next day

zu 15. Participial Constructions

Die Aufgabenstellung verlangt entweder Sätze zu verkürzen oder verkürzte Sätze aufzulösen.
Verkürzt werden Nebensätze durch Partizipien (sinngemäß: -ing oder -ed).
Sie erkennen Nebensätze an den Konjunktionen (z. B. »as«, »because« »since« → Grund; »when«, »after«, »while« → Zeit) bzw. den Relativpronomen »who«, »which« o. a.
Bei der Auflösung von Partizipialsätzen muß der Zusammenhang entscheiden, welche Möglichkeit sinnvoll ist (Grund; Zeit; . . .)
Die Zeitstufe des Nebensatzes hängt von der des Hauptsatzes ab.

zu 17. Adjective / Adverb

Die Aufgaben erscheinen als Lückentext. Die Wörter, um die es geht, stehen meist in Klammern.

Zur Wiederholung:

a) Das **Adjektiv** beschreibt das Substantiv (»the beautiful lady«; »She is beautiful«).
b) Das **Adverb** beschreibt ein Verb (»she sings beautifully«), ein Adjektiv (»She is extremely stupid«) bzw. ein anderes Adverb (»She sings extremely beautifully«).
c) Nach Verben, die einen Zustand oder eine Eigenschaft ausdrücken, stehen Adjektive, keine Adverbien (»It tastes good«; »It smells fresh«; »He looks tired«; »It sounds terrible«; »It feels hard«; »It is getting high«; »They are becoming more and more popular«).
d) Steigerung von Adjektiven:
   long → longer → longest;
   beautiful → more beautiful → most beautiful.
e) Steigerung von Adverbien:
   fast → faster → fastest;
   carefully → more carefully → most carefully.

zu 18. Relatives

Die Aufgaben erscheinen als Lückentext (Das geeignete Relativpronomen ist einzusetzen!) bzw. als Verknüpfung zweier Hauptsätze mit dem passenden Relativpronomen.

Achten Sie darauf, ob das Relativpronomen für Personen oder für Dinge stehen soll.

z.B. Tom met his friend, who had been ill.
My old car, which I sold last year, was an Austin.
He has to type out everything (which /that) a sighted teacher can write on the board (Relativpronomen kann wegfallen!).

zu 19. Reflexive / Reciprocal Pronouns

Vergleichen Sie bitte:

The girls see themselves (= sich selbst) in the mirror.

The girls smile at each other (= sich gegenseitig!).

Hilfen für die Übersetzung

zu 20. Translation

Die Übersetzung ist seit 1980 für alle Schüler verpflichtend.

Lernhilfen:

a) Lesen Sie den Text mehrmals gründlich durch und unterstreichen Sie problematische und unbekannte Wörter. Manchmal erbringt ein Blick auf den Gesamttext oder den anderen Aufgabenteil eine überraschende Lösung.

b) Die Übersetzung soll natürlich möglichst »wörtlich« sein und es dürfen keine sinntragenden Wörter ausgelassen werden. Dennoch muß Ihr Ziel ein flüssiger und stilistisch brauchbarer deutscher Text sein. Im Deutschen übliche Fremdwörter brauchen Sie nicht umständlich zu umschreiben (z. B. Hobby; Teenager; Fan).

c) Achten Sie besonders auf diese »Fehlerquellen«:

- **»Holprige« Satzstellung:**

  z. B. She arrived here from France a fortnight ago.
  → Sie kam vor 14 Tagen aus Frankreich hier an.
  The problem, however, is to write programmes.
  → Das Problem besteht jedoch darin, Programme zu schreiben.

- **Falscher Gebrauch der Zeitstufen,** v. a. Present Perfect:

  z. B. → We have been learning English for five years.
  → Wir lernen (schon) seit fünf Jahren Englisch.

- Schwierige **Passivsätze:**

  z. B. The children were shown films.
  → Man zeigte den Kindern Filme.

- **Leicht zu verwechselnde Wörter oder Ausdrücke:**

  z. B. to become = werden (nicht: bekommen!);
  for two days = 2 Tage lang (nicht: vor 2 Tagen!)
  at last = endlich; aber: at least = mindestens.

d) Achten Sie beim abschließenden Durchlesen darauf, daß Sie kein Wort oder gar einen ganzen Satz ausgelassen haben.
Da für jeden Satz eine gewisse Punktzahl vorgesehen ist (Einige Texte sind entsprechend abgedruckt!), bedeutet jeder brauchbare Lösungsvorschlag einen »Punktgewinn« für Sie!

Alphabetische Liste der schwierigen Wörter aus den Aufgabenstellungen

about	ungefähr
abstract noun	abstraktes Hauptwort
according	gemäß
active voice	Tatform, Aktiv
to add	hinzufügen
additional question	weiterführende Frage
adjective	Eigenschaftswort, Adjektiv
adverb	Umstandswort, Adverb
to answer	antworten
antonym	Wort mit entgegengesetzter Bedeutung
bold print	Fettdruck
brackets	Klammern
clause	Nebensatz
to compare	vergleichen
complete	vollständig
to complete	vervollständigen
correct	richtig
corresponding	entsprechend
each	jeder, jede, jedes
equivalent	Entsprechung
example	Beispiel
to explain	erklären
expression	Ausdruck
defective dialogue	Lückendialog
definition	Definition
different	verschieden
direct speech	direkte Rede
fact	Sachverhalt
false	falsch
to fill in	einsetzen
following	folgende
further	weitere
gap	Lücke
homophone	Wort mit gleicher Aussprache
true	richtig
if-clause	Bedingungssatz
italics	Kursivdruck
item	Punkt, Gedanke
to leave out	auslassen
to link	verbinden
main clause	Hauptsatz
meaning	Bedeutung
to mention	erwähnen
missing words	fehlende Worte
to name	nennen
negative sentence	verneinter Satz
noun	Hauptwort, Substantiv
opinion	Meinung
to pharaphrase	umschreiben
participial construction	Partizipialkonstruktion
passive voice	Leideform, Passiv
pronoun	Fürwort, Pronomen
to put into	setzen
really	wirklich
reason	Grund
reciprocal pronoun	Fürwort für Gegenseitigkeit
reflexive pronoun	rückbezügliches Fürwort
relative clause	Relativsatz
relative pronoun	Relativpronomen
to replace	ersetzen
report	Bericht
reported speech	indirekte Rede
to rewrite	nochmals schreiben
same	derselbe, dieselbe,
sentence	Satz
to shorten	verkürzen
similar	ähnlich
statement	Behauptung
suitable	passend
synonym	Wort mit gleicher Bedeutung
task	Aufgabe
tense	Zeit
to transform	umwandeln
to underline	unterstreichen
to use	benützen, gebrauchen
without	ohne

Number One For Books

1983 A

Failing an exam is not necessarily the end of the world. Sometimes it can even lead to success, as it did for the Foyle brothers.

Back in 1904, the sons of an East London grocer wanted to join the Civil Service. But William, aged nineteen, and his seventeen-year-old brother, Gilbert, never achieved that aim: they both failed the entrance examination. When the two brothers heard the disappointing exam results, they decided to sell their textbooks, which were no longer needed.

They put an advertisement in a student newspaper and were amazed by the number of replies they received from would-be buyers. Clearly, there was money to be made from selling books.

William and Gilbert Foyle began to buy old books from their friends, from market stalls, from second-hand shops . . . and to resell them.

For a while the two young men carried on their business part-time: during the day they had regular office jobs, limiting their book-selling activities to evenings and Sundays.

Within a year, however, they needed more time and more space: their rooms at home were bursting with books. That's why they went to Charing Cross Road – then, as now, the centre of London's book trade – and opened their first book shop there.

Today, Foyle's is said to be the world's largest bookshop. There are books everywhere: on the shelves, on the floor, on tables, on chairs, on counters . . . On its thirty miles of shelves it has millions of books. About twelve million books are sold each year – that is, over thirty-eight thousand a day (excluding Sundays).

Many of these sales are of quite common books: dictionaries, Shakespeare, the latest paperback. Others are more unusual: books on Japanese painting, Christianity in Central Africa, banana production. Right from the start, Foyle's earned the reputation of being able to supply almost any title.

Not all the stock is in English. In the vast foreign book department, the customer can find »Robin Hood« in Japanese, »Gone with the Wind« in Spanish, a James Bond thriller in Turkish . . . .

Customers are welcome at Foyle's, whether they really intend to buy books, just want to find some information, or whether they simply want to escape from a rainstorm. People can read a book through from cover to cover – if they don't mind standing!

Number One For Books

C	G	S/V

Which explanation best fits the underlined word or expression?
Mark it with a cross.

1. Clearly (line 10) means the same as — C: 1, G: –, S/V: –
   a) ☐ obviously
   b) ☐ in a clear manner
   c) ☐ easily understood
   d) ☐ completely

2. They carried on their business part-time (line 14) means the same as — C: 1, G: –, S/V: –
   a) ☐ During their business hours only one of them served customers.
   b) ☐ They were partners in the business.
   c) ☐ They did not work in their business the whole day.
   d) ☐ They sold books not only in the evenings and on Sundays.

3. Foyle's is said to be the world's largest bookshop (line 21) means the same as — C: 1, G: –, S/V: –
   a) ☐ Foyle's is thought to be the world's largest bookshop.
   b) ☐ Foyle's says that it is the world's largest bookshop.
   c) ☐ Foyle's is proud of being the world's largest bookshop.
   d) ☐ Foyle's pretends that it is the world's largest bookshop.

Replace the underlined expressions without changing the meaning of the sentence.

	C	G	S/V
4. The two brothers decided/ . . . to sell their textbooks. (line 8)	–	1	1
5. They were amazed/ . . . by the number of replies they	–	–	1
received/ . . . . (line 9/10)	–	–	1
6. About/ . . . twelve million books are sold each year. (line 24)	–	–	1
7. People can read a book through from cover to cover / . . . . (line 36/37)	–	–	2
8. Foyle's earned a reputation of being able to supply / . . . almost every title for their customers. (line 29)	–	–	1
9. Not all people visiting Foyle's really intend / . . . to buy books;	–	–	1
some just come in to escape / . . . a rainstorm. (line 34/36)	–	–	1

Finish the following sentences to explain the underlined expressions.

	C	G	S/V
10. A grocer (line 4) is a shopkeeper	1	1	1
11. Second-hand shops (line 13) are shops	1	1	1
12. A would-be buyer (line 10) is a person	1	1	1

Answer the following questions in complete sentences.
Questions on the Text. (Use your own words; if you copy the text word for word, you will lose points.)

	C	G	S/V
13. What is meant by ›number ONE for books‹?	1	1	1
14. What did the Foyle brothers have to do when they wished to join the Civil Service?	1	1	1
15. In what way did failing the entrance examination influence the Foyle brothers' lives?	1	1	1
16. What did the brothers have to do in order to have more time for their book selling activities?	1	1	1
17. Why does Foyle's Bookshop attract so many customers nowadays?	1	1	1

Further questions.	C	G	S/V
18. Why are dictionaries called common books in the text?	1	1	1
19. What sort of books do you like best, and why?	2	1	1
Monika's English friend Alan told her something about Foyle's. Use the elements given in brackets to complete the following sentences.			
20. Foyle's Bookshop . . . (found) in 1905.	–	1	–
21. The Foyle brothers . . . (never, think of, become) businessmen,	–	3	–
if they . . . (not, fail) their exam.	–	1	–
22. Their father . . . (want, they, join) the Civil Service.	–	3	–
23. Realizing that money . . . (can, make) from selling books	–	2	–
they . . . (not, hesitate) . . . (seize) the opportunity.	–	2	–
24. Since its foundation Foyle's . . . (achieve) a worldwide reputation.	–	1	–
Two students, Robert and Thomas, meet at Foyle's. Write down what Robert says.			
25. Robert: ». . .?« Thomas: »For two hours.«	1	1	1
26. Robert: ». . .?« Thomas: »No, I haven't. I've just looked at some books on London architecture. But they are too expensive for me.«	1	1	1
27. Robert: ». . .?« Thomas: »Of course, I did. But they've only got new ones at the moment.«	1	1	1

After having seen Foyle's Bookshop Monika couldn't help comparing it to her bookshop at home. Fill in the missing words.

	C	G	S/V
28. »I've been to a lot of bookshops, but this one is by far the . . . interesting.	–	1	–
29. Foyle's offers a . . . choice of books than my local bookshop.	–	1	–
30. My bookseller doesn't sell . . . . . . books . . . Foyles's and	–	3	–
he certainly earns much . . . than Foyle's does.	–	1	–

As the tourist sightseeing bus came up Charing Cross Road from Trafalgar Square, the guide pointed out Cambridge Circus and then, on the left, Foyle's bookshop. Translate into German what he said.

	C	G	S/V
31. »Ladies and gentlemen, may I have your attention, please? We are now passing Foyle's, one of the world's largest bookshops. It consists of the buildings with five storeys each. By the way, Foyle doesn't only deal in books; there is also a Foyle's Art Gallery and a video und record department. You will find that quite a few members of the staff are foreign students. So, no matter where you come from, you can be sure that there is always somebody available who speaks your own language. All the assistants have been instructed never to approach the customers but to wait until they are asked. So, if you are interested in books, believe me, there is no place like Foyle's.«	30	–	–

Can Australia's Aboriginals Teach Us Anything? 1983 B

Lately, some magazines – such as Newsweek – have reported, »Australia – dry as a bone«, and »Things are getting bad when the kangaroos start to die«.

Headlines of that kind generally do not impress us much, for to most Europeans the country ›down under‹ is just dry bushland and deserts. The truth, however, is that Australia is a country of almost unbelievable wealth and natural beauty. It is also a land of contrasts where unexpectedly long dry periods are followed by unforeseen floods.

In 1982, all the states except South Australia were suffering from a serious lack of rain.

Unlike white Australians, Aboriginals are used to these extreme conditions. Most of them still live in the ›outback‹, those remote areas which are the hottest and wildest places in the heart of Australia.

They are better than anyone else at finding food and water, because from childhood on they must learn how to survive. Aboriginals keep to their old customs and traditions.

Kath Walker, a famous Aboriginal writer, is immensely proud of her people and has worked to save their way of life and to prevent their country from being spoilt by modern man. In her books she tells us a story of her early life on an island close to the city of Brisbane:

»Dad taught us to hunt and fish when we were small but he told us to leave alone the protected animals and never kill for the sake of killing. We could all throw stones very straight, but my eldest brother was the best. He was a pretty good hunter even then. One day we went out hunting, trying to catch a wild pigeon. Unusually, the bird let us come very close. My brother threw the stone – and missed!

The pigeon flew away, and, at that very moment a kookaburra, which is a protected bird in Australia, laughed loudly in a tree above us. My brother shouted angrily and threw a stone with all his strength – and the kookaburra fell to the ground. We stood round in sudden silence: my brother had broken our law. We didn't notice our father coming towards us. When he saw the dead bird he looked terribly angry and sent us home. That evening he called us together. He did not ask any questions and we did not offer any excuses. He just said: ›You have killed for the sake of killing. For the next three months you are not allowed to hunt or fish. That is your punishment.‹«

Kath Walker wants to show us that the Aboriginals seem to know what we have obviously forgotten: that the only way to survive in this world is to stick to the law of nature.

Can Australia's Aboriginals Teach Us Anything?

Which explanation best fits the underlined word or expression?

	C	G	S/V
1. Lately (line 2) means the same as a) ☐ recently b) ☐ rather late c) ☐ in the end d) ☐ long ago e) ☐ shortly	1	–	–
2. all the states except South Australia (line 10) means the same as a) ☐ the whole of Australia b) ☐ all the states apart from South Australia c) ☐ all the states, especially South Australia d) ☐ a few Australian states.	1	–	–

Complete the following sentences by using words from the text.

	C	G	S/V
3. Very hot and dry areas are called . . .	–	–	1
4. . . . are the earliest inhabitants of a region.	–	–	1

Put the underlined parts into your own words.

	C	G	S/V
5. Large parts of Australia were suffering from lack of rain. (line 10/11)	2	1	1
6. protected animals (line 23)	1	1	1

Replace the underlined words or expressions without changing the meaning of the sentences.

	C	G	S/V
7. Headlines of that kind do not impress us much, for/ . . . to most Europeans the country is just dry bushlands and deserts. (lines 5–6)	–	–	1
8. Dry periods are followed by unforeseen floods. (line 9) Dry periods are followed by floods . . .	–	2	1
9. Most Aboriginals still live in those remote/ . . . areas. (line 13)	–	–	1
10. Father told us to leave alone/ . . . the protected animals. (lines 22/23)	–	1	1

Answer the following questions in complete sentences.

Questions on the Text. (Use your own words; if you copy the text word for word, you will lose points.)

	C	G	S/V
11. Why is it that dry periods cause hard times even for the Aboriginals?	1	1	1
12. How many brothers did Kath Walker have at least?	1	1	–
13. How does she try in her books to prevent her country from being spoilt by modern man?	1	1	1
14. Why is it important for Aboriginals to be able to throw stones straight?	1	1	1
15. What made the eldest brother break their law?	1	1	–

Further Questions.

	C	G	S/V
16. Why do you think most Aboriginals live in the wildest places in the heart of Australia?	1	1	2
17. How does modern man spoil nature? Give two examples.	2	1	2

Complete the following text by using the words in brackets in the proper form.	C	G	S/V
18. When we were children we learnt that we . . . (not, be allowed to) kill animals for the sake of killing.	–	1	–
19. Or father said, if we . . . (break) this law, no excuse	–	1	–
. . . (accept).	–	1	–
21. One morning my brothers and I . . . (go, hunt).	–	2	–
22. We . . . (not, have to) go far to find some birds we wanted for dinner.	–	1	–
23. My brother was very good . . . (throw) stones.	–	2	–
24. Therefore we expected . . . (he, kill) one of the birds.	–	2	–
25. But he . . . (not, be) very lucky.	–	1	–
26. In the afternoon, however, we discovered the . . .	–	1	–
27. (big) and . . . (beautiful) bird	–	1	–
28. we . . . (ever, see).	–	1	–
29. It . . . (not, notice) us	–	1	–
30. . . . (come).	–	1	–
31. My brother . . . (grow) more and more excited.	–	1	–
32. At last he . . . (slow) . . . (pick up) a stone and	–	2	–
33. threw it at the bird which . . . (fall) down	–	1	–
34. from the tree . . . (immediate).	–	1	–
35. . . . (unfortunate) he	–	1	–
36. . . . (kill) a protected bird.	–	1	–
Ask for the underlined parts of the sentences.			
37. Kath's father taught her to hunt and fish.	–	1	–
38. Her father taught her to hunt and fish.	–	1	–

Retell (in reported speech) what happened after the eldest brother had killed a kookaburra.

	C	G	S/V
39. Father only said to us: »Go home at once!«	–	2	–
40. We wondered: »What will our punishment be?«	–	1	–
41. I said: »We are all guilty. We have been hunting with you, so we will have to share the blame.«	–	4	–

Translate the following text into German.

	C	G	S/V
42. The Aboriginals have existed for over 25,000 years. During this time they have developed a lifestyle that is very different from European culture. They have never given up their old customs and this strong feeling for tradition prevents most of them from leaving their tribes. Those Aboriginals who move into white communities have a very difficult time. It requires great effort from both black and white Australians to co-exist peacefully. In the meantime, university courses run by Aboriginals have been introduced to educate white Australians about Aboriginal life. Exchange visits between white and Aboriginal children also help them to understand each other. Misunderstandings can only be overcome by good will on both sides. After all, the Aboriginals were there before the white man came.	30	–	–

C) Prüfungsaufgaben

1 Pedal Power 1982 A

Long, exhausting bicycle trips can give the rider, who isn't in training, pains throughout his body, sore hands, stiff shoulders and the general feeling that he'll never push a pedal again in his life.

The less ambitious cyclist, however, who doesn't want to pedal his way around the world, sees cycling from a different point of view.

It's one of the quickest, cheapest and simplest ways of getting around town, involving no tube or bus fares, and no parking problems. Above all, it's a good way of keeping fit – except in city traffic, where the cyclist can't avoid breathing in polluted air. With petrol prices increasing steadily, more and more people are taking to the saddle to cover short distances.

The bicycle is making a comeback at last. The vehicle has gone through many changes in size and design since the first real bicycle was made in 1840 by Kirkpatrick MacMillan, a Scottish blacksmith. He was so enthusiastic about the machine he had invented that he spent most of his time rushing round the town on it, so that eventually he had to be punished for »furious driving« on public roads. The people at that time couldn't imagine what the future held in store.

Although there is quite a difference between the early models and the racing bikes used by professional cyclists today, the design of the average bicycle hasn't much changed since the end of the 19th century, when a chain and rubber tyres were introduced.

By that time the bicycle had become an instrument of liberation. It enabled ordinary people to travel quickly to the next village and beyond, so that they learned about things outside their own small community. Cycling thus made it possible for them to go further afield to find jobs, or to attend schools, and in this way to widen their horizons. It soon became a very popular activity.

Even after the car arrived, people continued to own bicycles, but they became the poor relation of the car. They were only used by people who were unable to afford anything better. Cycling wasn't even a pleasure any more, as many motorists believed that the roads were for cars only.

To make cycling easier and safer today, it is absolutely necessary to increase the number of cycle paths running alongside ordinary roads. Then cyclists and motorists would no longer be such a danger to one another.

Pedal Power

	C	G	S/V
1.	1	–	–
2.	1	–	–
3.	1	–	–
4.	1	–	–

Mark the correct answer with a cross.

1. »More and more people are taking to the saddle« (line 11) means about the same as
   a) ☐ they are making the saddle more comfortable
   b) ☐ they are beginning to use bicycles
   c) ☐ they are transporting things to their bikes
   d) ☐ they are removing their saddles from the frames

2. »held in store« (line 19) means about the same as
   a) ☐ would keep till needed
   b) ☐ kept in a large shop
   c) ☐ kept behind curtains
   d) ☐ would bring

3. »by that time« (line 24) means about the same as
   a) ☐ before the end of the nineteenth century
   b) ☐ in 1842
   c) ☐ at the beginning of the twentieth century
   d) ☐ until 1900

4. »the average bicycle« (lines 21/22) means about the same as
   a) ☐ quite an old bicycle
   b) ☐ a very large bicycle
   c) ☐ a bicycle for aged persons
   d) ☐ the normal type of bicycle

Use the words of the same word families as the ones in brackets to fill the gaps.	C	G	S/V
5. It is hard to cycle to . . . (distance) places if you are not in training.	–	–	1
6. At first MacMillan's . . . (invent) was not a success, but it	–	–	1
showed his . . . (able) to construct good machines.	–	–	1
7. The . . . (introduce) of a chain and rubber tyres was an improvement.	–	–	1
8. Motorists are not too . . . (pleasure) when they are bothered by cyclists.	–	–	1
Fill in words or expressions with meanings similar to the ones underlined.			
9. Exhausting / . . . bicycle trips can give the rider / . . . pains throughout his body. (line 2)	–	–	1/1
10. In city traffic one can't avoid breathing in polluted / . . . air. (line 10)	–	–	1
11. Bikes were only used by people who were unable to afford /. . . anything better. (line 32)	–	1	1
Explain what is meant by			
12. a tube fare: (line 8)	1	1	1
13. a professional cyclist: (line 21)	1	1	1

	C	G	S/V
Answer the following questions in complete sentences.			
Questions on the Text: (Use your own words; if you copy the text word for word, you will lose points.)			
14. What are the disadvantages of travelling by bike in a city? (Name two.)	2	1	2
15. Why has the bicycle become so popular in recent years? (Give two reasons.)	2	1	1
16. What had to be done to improve MacMillan's bike? (Answer in the passive voice.)	1	2	1
Further questions.			
17. In what situation can a cyclist be a danger to a motorist?	1	1	2
18. What would you regard as ideal conditions for a cycling tour? (Name two items.)	2	1	1
After the ›Professional Road Race‹ you get the chance to ask one of the cyclists three questions. Use the elements given.			
19. when / career ». . .?«	1	1	1
20. incidents / race ». . .?«	1	1	1
21. time / daily training ». . .?«	1	1	1
Mark the word that does not rhyme.			
22. fare: ☐ bear ☐ fear ☐ fair ☐ where 23. quite: ☐ white ☐ quiet ☐ light ☐ height	–	–	2

Use the words in brackets in the proper form.	C	G	S/V
24. The . . . (early) you start learning to ride a bike,	–	1	–
the . . . (good).	–	1	–
25. On a bike you can get from one place to another			
(surprising/quick).	–	2	–
26. The plane is by far the . . . (fast), but also the . . .	–	1	–
. . . (expensive), of all means of transport.	–	1	–
27. As soon as you . . . (manage/keep) your balance, you are	–	1	–
on the point of . . . (be) able . . . (ride) a bike.	–	2	–
28. The cyclist . . . (can/not/avoid) . . . (be) exposed to bad	–	2	–
weather.			
29. Storms and rain . . . (not/prevent) some people from . . . (go)	–	1	–
on bicycle tours.	–	1	–
The head boy of a school writes to the Mayor of his town. Complete the following letter.			
Dear Sir,			
30. As you know, many pupils in our town cycle to school every			
morning. Last week a boy from our school . . . (injure/serious)	–	2	–
on his way to school.			
31. Years ago you . . . (promise) that a cycle path . . . (build)	–	3	–
alongside the main road.			
32. So far nothing . . . (happen).	–	1	–
33. For us cycling would be more fun and safer if we . . . (have)	–	1	–
a lane of our own.			
34. We hope that something . . . (do) soon.	–	2	–
Yours sincerely, Tom Smith			
35. **Translate from line 24** »By that time . . .« **to line 33** ». . . cars only«.	29	–	–
(Die Wörter ›liberation‹, ›job‹, ›popular‹, ›activity‹ dürfen nicht als Fremdwörter übernommen werden.)			

Only One Problem — 1982 B

I was nervous as I stood in front of the Head Office in London; the firm had a high international reputation – and the thought of joining the company made me more excited. I had taken a great deal of care with my appearance. I was wearing my best suit with the right tie and pocket handkerchief; my shoes were smartly polished, my teeth were well brushed and I was wearing my best smile.

A man in a smart uniform courteously opened the large doors for me, and as I approached the receptionist's desk she smiled quite pleasantly. »Good morning.« Raising her eye-brows, she inquired politely whether she could help me. »Good morning«, I replied. »My name is Jenkins. I am here for an interview with Mr Symonds.« At that, the receptionist's smile suddenly disappeared. She looked into a long diary, picked up the telephone and spoke quietly into it, cupping her hand round the mouthpiece and turning her back on me as she did so.

»Will you come this way?« She set off down a wide corridor, her back straight and stiff with disapproval. We entered an automatic lift: the girl remained silent and unfriendly and avoided looking at me. She showed me into a room, told me to wait there and then quickly returned to the lift. After a few minutes I was asked into a large room, where four men were seated at a long table.

One of them, Mr Symonds, shook hands with me and introduced his colleagues, and then offered me a chair. After asking a few short questions about my place of birth and experience in the Air Force, they began to question me closely on telecommunications and the developments of electronics in that field. Suddenly my nervousness disappeared: now I was confident, because it was a familiar subject.

And then it was all over. Mr Symonds looked at his colleagues. They nodded to him, and he said: »Mr Jenkins, we are completely satisfied with your replies and are convinced that your qualifications, ability and experience make you perfectly suitable for the post we have in mind. But we are faced with a certain difficulty. Employing you would mean placing you over a number of our English employees, many of whom have been with us a very long time. We feel that such an appointment would harm the good relations which have always existed in this firm. So I'm afraid we shall not be able to use you.« At this he rose, and offered me his hand to shake as a polite way of dismissing me.

I felt exhausted, weak and confused: yet somehow I managed to leave that office and walked out into the busy sunlit street. I had just been brought face to face with something I had either forgotten or completely ignored during the last six successful years – my black skin.

Only One Problem	C	G	S/V
Mark the correct answer with a cross.			
1. A firm with »a high international reputation« (line 3) a) ☐ has employees from other countries b) ☐ has difficulty in finding highly qualified employees c) ☐ is very well thought of in England and abroad d) ☐ can offer interesting jobs to foreigners	1	–	–
2. He »had taken a great deal of care with his appearance« (lines 4/5) because he wanted a) ☐ to show off b) ☐ to make a good impression c) ☐ to appear intelligent d) ☐ to give the impression that he was rich	1	–	–
3. When Mr Symonds »offered me his hand to shake as a polite way of dismissing me« (lines 36/37) a) ☐ he wanted to congratulate me b) ☐ he showed his disappointment c) ☐ he wanted to ask me to leave d) ☐ he intended to apologize	1	–	–
4. »courteously« (line 8) means the same as a) ☐ shortly b) ☐ silently c) ☐ politely d) ☐ quickly	1	–	–

Which phrase in the text tells you that . . .

	C	G	S/V
5. the receptionist didn't like Mr Jenkins? (one example)	1	–	–
6. it was a bright day with a great deal of traffic?	2	–	–

Complete the following sentences by using words of the same family.

	C	G	S/V
7. Mr Jenkins was filled with great . . . (excited) and the . . .	–	–	1
(silent) in the room made him nervous.	–	–	1
8. Mr Symonds and his colleagues listened to his replies with			
great . . . (satisfied) and were convinced that he was . . .	–	–	1
(qualifications) for the job.	–	–	1

Replace the underlined words or phrases by words of your own, without changing the meaning of the sentences.

	C	G	S/V
9. Mr Symonds began to question me closely (line 24/25)			
Mr Symonds began to question me . . .	–	1	1
10. The developments in electronics were a familiar subject to Mr Jenkins. (lines 25/27)			
Mr Jenkins . . . the developments in electronics.	–	1	1
11. In the end Mr Symonds said: »You are suitable for the post we have in mind.« (line 31)			
»You are suitable for the post we . . .«	–	1	1

	C	G	S/V
Answer the following questions in complete sentences. Don't begin your answers with ›because‹.			
Questions on the Text. (Use your own words; if you copy the text word for word, you will lose points.)			
12. Why did the receptionist suddenly become unfriendly?	1	1	1
13. What had Mr Jenkins done to look smart? (One item only)	1	1	1
14. Why did the receptionist hold her hand round the mouthpiece while telephoning?	1	2	1
Further questions.			
15. What do you think the receptionist said over the phone to Mr Symonds?	1	1	1
16. Why do you think Mr Jenkins got the interview with Mr Symonds but not the job?	2	1	1
17. What kind of job have you already applied for or do you intend to apply for? (Give a reason.)	1	2	2
18. This is the symbol of a well-known organization in Great Britain. What do you think it means?	1	1	1
What Mr Jenkins was thinking (Use the correct tenses.)			
19. On his way to the firm he said to himself, »Well, if I . . . (not/get) that job, there . . . (be) two more chances remaining.«	–	2	–
20. After the interview he thought, »If my black skin . . . (matter)	–	1	–
in the past, I . . . (not/enjoy) the six exciting and successful years.«	–	1	–

	C	G	S/V
Complete the following text with the correct forms of the words in brackets, making all necessary changes.			
21. Mr Jenkins, a coloured person, . . . (fail/get) a job last week.	–	2	–
22. Although he was . . . (high) intelligent and most suited for the	–	1	–
job, he . . . (not/accept) for it.	–	2	–
23. By . . . (refuse) to offer this person employment, the firm has	–	1	–
violated the Race Relations Act, which . . . (exist) for sixty	–	1	–
years now.			
24. This Act protects everybody from . . . (to be discriminated)	–	1	–
against because of his colour, race or nationality.			
25. When we . . . (hear) about Mr Jenkins' case, we . . . (advise)	–	2	–
him . . . (complain) . . . (immediate).	–	2	–
Write your personal letter of application for a job, containing the following points:			
26. introduction/age/school attended/reasons for applying to that particular firm/interests/polite close			
Dear Sir, ... / Yours faithfully, ...	6	6	6
If Mr Jenkins had been accepted, he would have received a letter like the following. Translate it into German.			
27. Dear Mr Jenkins,			
As a result of the interview on 26th May, we are glad to offer you the post you applied for.			
Because of your high standard of education and your great experience, we are completely convinced that we can work together most satisfactorily.			
If you should need any further information on salary, working conditions* or other matters, please do not hesitate to contact our Mr Smith as soon as possible.			
You are kindly requested to return the work contract* with your signature by 1st July at the latest.	27	–	–
We look forward to seeing you,			
Yours sincerely,			
G. W. Symonds			

* Diese Wörter dürfen nicht als Fremdwörter übernommen werden.

The Driving Test

1981 A

With a silent prayer, she did as she had been taught: she put the car in the first gear, checked the mirror, looked over her right shoulder, signalled that she was about to move off, released the handbrake and stepped on the accelerator. Nothing happened.

Knowing how nervous driving-test candidates feel, the examiner suggested gently: »Now take your time, and let's start all over again.«

Blushing she started the engine this time, and sailed through her test without making further mistakes.

Situations like that may occur all over the world, and taking a driving test has always been an exciting experience. In 1979, more than a million and a half learners took the test in Great Britain – more than half of them failed. A recent analysis showed that in one out of every nine failed tests, the examiner had to take over the braking or steering to prevent an accident.

This relatively high failure rate may be due to the British system of getting a driving licence. Of course, there are many driving schools in Britain, but nobody is obliged to take driving lessons there. You can acquire all your skills in any car you like and can be taught by your friends or relatives.

Before starting out, however, a learner driver must obtain a provisional licence. This gives him the right to drive on all British roads except motorways, as long as he is accompanied and advised by a person who holds a full British licence. In addition he has to put L-plates (»L« for »learner«) on the front and rear of the car. The provisional licence costs £ 2 and is valid for a year.

Statistics prove that too many learners take the test without being thoroughly prepared. Because of a shortage of examiners and the high failure rate, there is a waiting-list of 800,000 candidates. In London, candidates have to wait from six to ten months on average until they are admitted to the test.

You can even take your test in your own car. If you want to do so, check it over carefully. Otherwise you might not get your driving licence, for the simple reason that your car might break down. This was the case when a theoretically and practically well-prepared candidate set off on the test-drive. After a few miles the engine suddenly stopped, and examiner and candidate had to walk home together in the rain.

The Driving Test

Which is the best explanation? Mark the correct answer with a cross.

1. »Blushing« (line 8) means about the same as
   a) turning round
   b) being puzzled
   c) turning red
   d) correcting herself

2. »To prevent an accident« (line 15) means
   a) to avoid an accident
   b) to cause an accident
   c) to be involved in an accident
   d) to expect an accident

3. There is a »high failure rate« (line 16) means that a great number of people
   a) do not pass the test
   b) pass the test
   c) take the test
   d) do not come to the test

Fill in the proper words. (Use three words from the list below.)

4. In school, we have . . . from 9.30 to 9.45.
5. This car is for . . . .
6. You must . . . a minute.
   (brake, sail, break, rain, weight, reign, sale, wait)

Use the nouns corresponding to the verbs.

7. What is your . . . (suggest)?
8. He has a weak heart and should avoid any . . . (excite).
9. The examiner must have . . . (prove) that a candidate can drive.

	C	G	S/V
1.	1	–	–
2.	1	–	–
3.	1	–	–
4.	1	–	–
5.	1	–	–
6.	1	–	–
7.	–	–	1
8.	–	–	1
9.	–	–	1

	C	G	S/V
Fill in words or expressions with meanings similar to the ones underlined.			
10. The examiner suggested gently/ . . . : »Now take your time.«	–	–	1
11. Situations like that may occur/ . . . all over the world.	–	–	1
12. There is a shortage of/ . . . examiners.	–	–	2
13. The candidate was told to start all over again/	–	–	2
Complete the following sentences by using the opposites of the underlined words.			
14. 52 per cent of the candidates failed; the other 48 per cent . . . the test.	–	–	1
15. Some candidates prepare for the test very thoroughly; most of them, however, do it rather	–	–	1
16. The examiner said: »Take your time.« He didn't say: ». . .«.	–	–	1
Questions on the Text. **Answer the following questions in complete sentences.**			
17. What does it mean if you see a car with L-plates on the front and rear?	1	1	1
18. Why did nothing happen the first time the candidate tried to drive away?	1	1	–
19. What is a learner not allowed to do? (Name two things)	2	1	1
20. What can English candidates do if they want to get their driving licence without taking driving lessons?	1	1	1

	C	G	S/V
Additional questions.			
21. On which side of an English car does the driver sit? Say why.	2	1	1
22. Why does a driver have to check the mirror before he starts?	1	1	1
23. What should you do if you see an accident?	1	1	1
Explain in complete English sentences what the following German road signs mean.			
24. »Vehicles . . . .«	1	–	1
25. »Drivers . . . ,«	1	–	1
Complete the following sentences, using the words in brackets in their correct form.			
This is how you should prepare for the driving test in Great Britain:			
26. Check that your eyesight . . . (meet) the . . . (require)	–	1	–
standard.	–	1	–
27. Make sure your provisional licence is up to date and . . . (sign).	–	1	–
28. Do not drink beforehand; if the examiner . . .	–	1	–
(notice) that you . . . (drink) anything at all,	–	1	–
he . . . (not, allow) you to drive.	–	1	–
29. Remember that you . . . (ask) questions on traffic regulations.	–	1	–
30. Do not give up if you make a mistake. The thing to do is to keep on . . . (drive, normal).	–	2	–

	C	G	S/V
Rewrite the following sentences, replacing the -ing construction with a clause in each case.			
31. Knowing how nervous candidates feel, the examiner suggested another try.	–	2	–
32. Before starting out, a learner driver must obtain a licence.	–	1	–
Fill in the gaps with the correct forms of the words in brackets.			
33. The candidate's . . . (practical) work was . . . (weak) than his theoretical knowledge.	–	2	–
34. He had prepared for the test quite . . . (careful)	–	1	–
and so he passed it . . . (easy).	–	1	–
Say the same thing, using a different construction.			
35. In England, you can be taught how to drive by your friends. —— In England your friends . . .	–	1	–
36. A learner driver has to put an L-plate on the car. An L-plate	–	1	–
37. The police stopped him for driving too fast. He	–	1	–
Fill in the gaps, using other expressions for the ones underlined.			
38. – In England, we <u>are obliged to</u> keep to the left. – In Germany we aren't. We . . . keep to the right.	–	1	–
39. – In Germany, we <u>are obliged to</u> wear safety belts. What about you? —— In England we aren't. We . . . wear them if we don't want to.	–	1	–
40. – <u>Are</u> you <u>able to</u> drive a car? – Of course, I am. But I . . . drive a lorry.	–	1	–
41. Translate from line 26 to line 37.	25	–	–

Au-Pair Girls **1981 B**

Thirty thousand au-pair girls come to Britain every year. They offer their help, and in exchange they hope to get a chance to improve their English and to get to know the English way of life.

The relationship between the housewife and her au-pair is whatever they make it. Some girls have to work all day long – a few even say they are treated like slaves! Most of them, however, have a reasonable amount of free time, which they can use as they like. Marianne, for example, an 18-year-old German girl, works six hours a day, helping in the household, collecting the children from school and looking after them when their parents are away. She sleeps in the family's guestroom, with an extra bed for girlfriends to stay overnight. Marianne is quite happy now, but the job she had before was a very bad experience: »My host family rarely talked to me,« she said, »and they wouldn't let me have friends in. I was very lonely. Moreover, I had to look after a mentally handicapped child – which my host family hadn't told me before I arrived. After a month I left, because the work was too hard for me, and I had too many disagreements with the parents about money and working conditions.«

So why is it that a lot of girls keep coming and are attracted by the adventure of being an au-pair? Many hope their English will help them find better jobs at home as secretaries or receptionists. Some are just filling in time before they get married.

How do you find a place as an au-pair? The best way is either through personal recommendation or by enquiring at a British Consulate, where they have a charter laying down an au-pair's rights and duties, which may vary considerably. Knowing that difficulties may arise, the Government has expressed the hope that an au-pair will be treated like a »daughter of the house«. The golden rule is not to ask her to do anything one wouldn't do oneself.
In general, an au-pair should be given a room to herself, one and a half free days a week and sufficient pocket money. As a rule she will have most of her meals with the family, and there should be time for her to attend English language classes, go out in the evening, and enjoy herself with her friends.

Au-Pair Girls

	C	G	S/V
Complete the following sentences with suitable words from the text.			
1. When we go to the station to meet someone and bring him home, we . . . him.	1	–	–
2. If I often argue with a friend about differences of opinion, I have . . . with him.	1	–	–
3. A . . . is someone who welcomes guests to a hotel.	1	–	–
4. A . . . is someone who receives visitors to his home.	1	–	–
Fill in words with meanings similar to the ones underlined.			
5. Many girls hope to get a chance to improve their English during their stay in Great Britain. (line 3) But very often it takes rather a long time to . . . the language	–	–	2
6. Marianne's first host family rarely talked to her. (line 14) That's why she . . . had an opportunity to practise her English.	–	–	1
7. The work was too hard for her. (line 18) She had not thought that it would be so	–	–	1
8. Many girls get sufficient pocket-money (line 32), so that they even have . . . money to buy little presents for the children.	–	–	1
Fill in words belonging to the same word family.			
9. There are au-pair girls who are **treated** like slaves; they deserve better	–	–	1
10. Quite a number of them, who are usually not **married,** go to Britain just to fill in time before their	–	–	1
11. If the girls don't **know** English well, they attend evening classes to improve their . . . of the language.	–	–	1
12. The English way of **life** is different from the way German people	–	–	1

Answer the following questions in complete sentences. Questions on the Text.	C	G	S/V
13. What jobs does Marianne do, apart from working in the household? Give two items.	2	1	–
14. Name two reasons why she was not happy in her first host family?	2	1	–
15. How long did Marianne stay at her first place?	1	1	–
16. How can a girl get addresses of host families in England?	1	1	–
17. What is a host family supposed to offer an au-pair girl in exchange for her work? Name two items in one sentence.	2	1	–
Further questions.			
18. Why do you think families take au-pair girls? Give two reasons.	2	2	1
19. Apart from going abroad, what can you do after leaving school if you don't want to forget your English?	1	1	1
20. Why is it an advantage for you to know English? Give two reasons.	2	1	2
Imagine you have just arrived in England. Tell your host family in one sentence each – mentioning the details given in brackets – about ...			
21. ... your journey (means of transport, time taken)	1	2	1
22. ... your plans for your next holiday (place, activities).	1	1	1

	C	G	S/V
Mark the WRONG words in each of the following sentences with a cross.			
23. Marianne and her first host family didn't get on well with	1	–	–
☐ herself.			
☐ themselves.			
☐ each other.	1		
24. Marianne had not imagined ☐ herself		–	–
☐ themselves			
☐ each other			
that the job would be so hard.	1		
25. Her second host family, however, took her to many parties,		–	–
where they enjoyed ☐ herself tremendoùsly.			
☐ themselves			
☐ each other			
In her first letter home, Marianne tells her family what she was asked on her arrival by her host mother. Rewrite the questions in indirect speech.			
She asked me . . .			
26. (»Is there anything you don't eat?«)	–	3	–
27. (»Do you plan to go to a language school?«)	–	2	–
28. (»Where did you learn your English?«)	–	2	–
29. (»When do you want your day off?«)	–	2	–

Rewrite the following sentences, replacing the participial constructions.

	C	G	S/V
30. One should read the charter **laying** down an au-pairs rights and duties.	–	2	–
31. **Not knowing** anything about the charter, Marianne went to the British Consulate.	–	3	–
32. The list of host families **given** to her was quite promising.	–	2	–
33. **Asked** why she wanted to work as an au-pair, she said she wanted to get to know England.	–	2	–

A lady named Mrs Sheila Steward,
who has experience with au-pair girls,
writes a letter to a friend of hers, Mrs Peggy Gibbs.

34. Translate her letter into German.

	C	G	S/V
Dear Peggy,			
A little while ago, you wrote that you would like an au-pair girl.	2	–	–
Well, we have now got one.	1	–	–
She is called Marie, and she arrived here from France a fortnight ago.	2	–	–
Our first impression of her was not very promising. When we collected her from the airport, she didn't look very sure of herself, and we were afraid that she wouldn't prove suitable for the job.	5	–	–
Perhaps this was due to the fact that it's the first time she has been away from home, and her knowledge of English is rather limited.	6	–	–
Meanwhile she has turned out to be a great help.	2	–	–
Marie is good with the children and doesn't need to be told what to do.	2	–	–
Why don't you come and meet her next weekend?	1	–	–
Love, Sheila	1	–	–

Click Your Fingers 1980 A

When Andrew Godfrey was an 11-year-old pupil at Dorton School he wrote an essay called »Why I Dislike School«.
The title was ironic. It was clear from every sentence that he loved school, and fifteen years later, in spite of having been born totally blind, he became a teacher at a school for sighted children.

Andrew, who studied at Oxford, teaches French and German at Ashford College in Middlesex. It was a risk for the headmaster to employ a blind teacher: parents might have objected, and children could have taken advantage of his inability to see them. But if you visit one of his lessons you will immediately realise why he has been successful.

The secret of his success is his enthusiasm and sense of humour. Of course, he has to prepare his lessons very thoroughly. Instead of the blackboard he uses an overhead projector. He has to type out in advance everything a sighted teacher can write on the board during the lesson.

When answers must be written on the blackboard, Andrew asks one of the youngsters to do the job. Couldn't this cause problems? »Yes, of course,« he admits. »But you can bet your life that if there are thirty pairs of eyes to find the slightest error, mistakes are not common.« In any case, he checks the blackboard work frequently by having it spelt out aloud.

At the beginning, one difficulty was that the pupils automatically put up their hands to draw his attention. Of course, he had to say, »I can't see you and it will just make your arms ache!« He suggested another method. The children click their fingers, and he can tell who they are by where the sound comes from. Practice has given him the ability to recognise one clicker in a row of six. This is all the more surprising when you learn that he is deaf in one ear.

For correcting homework Andrew has a number of voluntary helpers. He has proved that you don't need to be able to see to become a successful teacher of sighted children.

Click Your Fingers

C | L

Which is the best explanation?
Write down the number and letter.

1. »Parents might have objected« (line 9) means — C: 1 | L: –
   a) they might have protested
   b) they might have been puzzled
   c) they might have been glad
   d) they might have agreed
   e) they might have hesitated

2. If you »take advantage« (line 10) of something — C: 1 | L: –
   a) you do it in advance
   b) you take somebody's advice
   c) you try to profit from it
   d) you improve it
   e) you miss a chance

3. »You can bet your life« (line 20) means — C: 1 | L: –
   a) you can make your life easier
   b) you can live better
   c) you certainly can't believe it
   d) you can make your life worse
   e) you can be quite sure

Complete the following sentences using opposites.
Write down the words only.

4. Andrew has to prepare his lesson **thoroughly.**
   He can't afford to prepare them . . . . — C: 1 | L: 1
5. He does not **deny** that he sometimes has problems.
   He . . . that his position is difficult. — C: 1 | L: 1

	C	L
Replace the underlined words without changing the meaning of the sentences. Write down the words only		
6. He was born totally blind.	1	1
7. The answers must be written.	1	1
8. They find the slightest error.	1	1
9. . . . when you learn that he is deaf in one ear. (line 30)	1	–
Complete the following sentences. Do not use words of the same family.		
10. If a person is deaf he or she . . .	1	1
11. Voluntary helpers are people who help him . . .	1	2
Questions on the text (Answer in complete sentences.)		
12. How old was Andrew Godfrey when he started teaching?	1	1
13. Why did the pupils automatically put up their hands to draw his attention?	1	2
14. What difficulties does a blind teacher have which a teacher who can see does not have? (Write two facts.)	2	1
15. In what ways is Andrew Godfrey assisted by his pupils? (Write two facts.)	2	2
16. In what ways does Andrew find out what his pupils write on the board?	1	2
Additional questions (Answer in complete sentences.)		
17. What did Andrew have to do to qualify for university?	1	2
18. What problems do blind people have in everyday life? (Write two examples.)	2	4

Defective dialogue

A reporter goes to Ashford College and asks a pupil some questions about Mr. Godrey. Write them down.

	C	L
19. Reporter: ». . .?« Pupil: »Yes, I know him. He is my teacher.«	1	1
20. Reporter: ». . .?« Pupil: »French and German.«	1	2
21. Reporter: ». . .?« Pupil: »Not at all. The lessons go very well.«	1	2
22. Reporter: ». . .?« Pupil: »Well, we click our fingers as a sign.«	2	2

Rewrite the following sentences. Use the words in brackets and add any other words that are necessary.

	C	L
23. He . . . (be) blind . . . many years now.	–	2
24. Although he was blind, he . . . (give) a job by the headmaster.	–	2
25. After . . . (leave) university, he began to teach.	–	1
26. Mr Godfrey would not be able to correct the pupils' homework if they . . . (not, help) him.	–	2
27. Instead of . . . (write) on the blackboard he uses an overhead projector.	–	1
28. Pupils . . . are in contact with handicapped people can understand problems better . . . others.	–	2
29. I showed a . . . (blind) the way to a park for	–	1
the . . . (blind).	–	1

	C	L
Rewrite the following sentence, replacing the -ing form by a clause.		
30. There are thirty pairs of eyes acting as my eyes. (lines 20/21)	–	2
Rewrite the following sentence starting with »Although he . . . «		
31. In spite of having been born totally blind be became a teacher.	–	1
Which word can be inserted after »everything«?		
32. He has to type out in advance everything a sighted teacher can write on the board. (lines 15/16)	–	1
Translate the following text.		
(Die unterstrichenen Wörter dürfen nicht als Fremdwörter übernommen werden.)		
33. It was not easy for Andrew to become a teacher.	2	–
He was told that he would have great difficulty in getting a job./	4	–
He was not willing to give up, however, and at last managed to get accepted at Oxford.	5	–
But when he began to apply for a position, schools refused him with excuses such as: »We have too many steps.«	5	–
One headmaster said, »I'm putting myself in your place.	3	–
Would I be able to teach with my eyes closed?«	3	–
We can understand the headmaster's doubts./	2	–
But we ourselves are in danger of being blind towards the problems of handicapped people.	5	–

Does Travel Broaden The Mind? 1980 B

You very often hear it said that travel broadens the mind: if you stay in your own country the whole time, your ideas remain narrow, whereas, if you travel, you see new customs, eat new foods, do new things, and come back home with a broader mind.

But does this always happen? An acquaintance of mine, Mr. Low, who lives in England and had never been outside the country until last summer, decided to have a short holiday in France. When he returned, I asked him what he had thought of it. »Terrible,« was his answer.

»I couldn't get a nice cup of tea anywhere. Thank goodness I'm back.«

I asked him: »Didn't you have any good food while you were in France?«

»Oh, the dinners were all right,« he said. »I found a little place where they did quite good fish and chips – not as good as ours, mind you, but they weren't bad. But the breakfasts were terrible: no bacon, no sausages, no tomatoes and no fried bread. I did in fact have fried eggs and chips, but it was quite a business getting them to cook them. They expected me to eat rolls, and when I asked for marmalade, they brought strawberry jam. The trouble is they don't know any English.«

»But didn't you eat any of the famous French food?«

»What? Me?« he said. »Of course not! Give me good old English food every time.«

Obviously travel had not broadened his mind. He had gone to France determined to live there exactly as if he were in England, and had judged it entirely from his English point of view.

On the other hand there are some travellers who accept and even imitate all foreign customs and habits without question. They demand spaghetti with every meal; they take a siesta in the afternoon, and they use foreign words in every other sentence.

Perhaps the ideal thing would be if travel could succeed in making people become more tolerant of other people's way of life without giving up their own.

Does Travel Broaden The Mind? C L

Which is the best explanation?
Write down the number and letter.

1. »They expected me to eat . . .« (line 17) means 1 –
   a) they made me eat . . .
   b) they accepted that I ate . . .
   c) I ate everything except . . .
   d) they forced me to eat . . .
   e) they wanted me to eat . . .

2. »He had judged it . . .« (line 25) means 1 –
   a) he had enjoyed it
   b) he had seen no justice in it
   c) he had justified it
   d) he had found the solution
   e) he had formed his opinion

3. »Some people use foreign words in every other sentence« (line 29) suggests the idea 1 –
   a) they use them in different sentences
   b) they use them in one of the following sentences
   c) they use them in every second sentence
   d) they use them in all the other sentences
   e) they use them in another sentence

What are they made from? Complete the sentences.
Write down the missing words only.

4. »chips« (line 13) are made from . . . 1 –
5. »bread« (line 15) is made from . . . 1 –

Complete the following sentences using the opposites of the underlined words. You need only write the missing words.

	C	L
6. Obviously travel had not broadened Mr. Low's mind. He remained . . .-minded.	1	–
7. Many people are dissatisfied with their . . . country and try to leave it for foreign lands.	1	–

Replace the underlined words without changing the meaning of the sentences.
Write down the words/expressions only.

	C	L
8. He had never been outside the country. (line 7)	1	1
9. It was quite a business. (line 16)	1	1
10. Mr. Low had judged France entirely from his English point of view. (line 25)	1	1

Complete these sentences.

	C	L
11. If you are tolerant you . . .	1	2
12. If you imitate a person you . . .	1	2

Questions on the text. (Answer in complete sentences.)

	C	L
13. What was Mr. Low's opinion of the meals he had in France? (Give two examples.)	2	1
14. Why did they bring Mr. Low jam instead of marmalade?	1	2
15. What, apart from the food problem, made travelling in France difficult for him?	1	2

Additional questions. (Answer in complete sentences.)

	C	L
16. What, in your opinion, did Mr. Low expect in France?	1	1
17. Why do some people imitate foreign habits after having returned from a journey?	1	2
18. How can you prepare for a journey to a foreign country if you want to enjoy it as much as possible? (Find two ways.)	2	4

Defective dialogue.

C L

During his holiday in France Mr. Low always goes to the same restaurant. Two waiters are talking about their English guest. Write down what waiter A says.

19. Waiter A: ». . .?« 1 1
    Waiter B: »The same as usual. He never touches French food.«
20. Waiter A: ». . .?« 1 2
    Waiter B: »No, I don't think so. In fact, I'm sure he won't.«
21. Waiter A: ». . .?« 1 2
    Waiter B: »No, not so far; not even one franc.«
22. Waiter A: ». . .?« 1 1
    Waiter B: »No. Fortunately he is the only one of that kind.«

A Rather Strange Experience.
The author told a friend about the following conversation with his acquaintance, Mr. Low.
Write down this report in indirect speech.

23. Mr. Low said: »I couldn't get a nice cup of tea anywhere.« – 2
24. I asked him: »Didn't you have any good food while you were in France?« – 3
25. He said: »I'll take some English food with me next time.« – 3

Rough Sea.
Rewrite the following description of Mr. Low's Channel crossing last summer.

26. After the boat left Newhaven, it . . . (strike) by a storm. – 2
    The waves . . . (be) so gigantic that the passengers . . . – 1
    (throw) against the railing. – 2
    There was nothing that . . . (can, do) to stop the ship . . . (roll). – 3
    . . . (feel) thirsty, Mr. Low . . . (decide, go) to the cafeteria – 2
    . . . (buy) a cup of coffee. – 1
    Unfortunately, he . . . (not even, manage) to reach the stairs – 1
    . . . (lead) down to the cafeteria, because seasickness . . . – 1
    (overcome) him. – 1

Translate the following text.

	C	L
27. In Italy, I once met a German tourist who behaved like the Englishman in the story.	4	–
It was not easy for him to find a hotel, as he did not speak Italian.	4	–
He was not willing to learn the language, because most Italians in the holiday areas speak German.	4	–
He was sometimes told that all the hotels were full, while an Italian tourist who arrived later managed to find a room.	5	–
Of course, tourists have no possiblitiy of mastering a foreign language in a few weeks, but this is an obvious excuse: they	7	–
would be able to enjoy their holidays much better if they attended courses before going abroad.	4	–

A Friendly People 1979 A

The Americans are said to be extremely helpful, especially towards neighbors and fellow-citizens. There are good historical reasons for this. American colonists and pioneers learned to depend on one another for assistance and protection during times of crisis. They simply had to – if they wanted to stay alive. In modern everyday life there are still many ways in which Americans are ready to lend each other a helping hand.

Here is a practical example to show how friendly and helpful they can be. Mara Czerny, a young woman from Czechoslovakia, lives in a small town in the Middle West. Like many immigrants, she has unlimited faith in the goodwill of Americans. One summer afternoon, however, it seemed that this faith was going to be disappointed.

Mara was enjoying a picnic with a group of friends, when suddenly she got up and rushed off to find a telephone. On returning she explained, »I just remembered that I left a chicken roasting in the oven. So I called the Fire Department and asked them to send someone round to turn off the stove.«

The others tried to convince Mara that this was not exactly the Fire Department's function, not even in America. Probably a fireman would go to Mara's apartment, they said, but only to make sure that nothing had caught fire. Afterwards she would be accused of using electricity in a thoughtless way, and in addition she would almost certainly have to pay all the Fire Department's costs.

But that evening Mara's faith was fully justified. When the party arrived at Mara's apartment to see what had happened, they looked at each other in amazement. Not only had the fireman turned off the stove when the chicken was done, but he had made a delicious salad to go with it. On the table (next to the recipe for the salad) he had left a polite note warning her against future carelessness.

A Friendly People

C | L

Read the following explanations and write down the number and letter of the best one in each case.

1. »She would be accused of ...« (line 22) suggests the following idea: 1 –
   a) Man würde sie verachten ...
   b) Man würde sie tadeln ...
   c) Man würde sie beschuldigen ...
   d) Man würde sie bestrafen ...

2. »Her faith was fully justified« (line 25) suggests the following idea: 1 –
   a) Sie glaubte an das Gesetz.
   b) Ihr Glaube wurde bestätigt.
   c) Sie glaubte an die Gerechtigkeit.
   d) Ihr Glaube wurde erschüttert.

3. »To lend someone a helping hand« (line 7/8) means 1 –
   a) to shake hands with somebody.
   b) to lend a person something.
   c) to borrow something from a person.
   d) to assist someone.

4. »The chicken was done« (line 28) means 1 –
   a) the chicken was finished.
   b) the chicken was burnt.
   c) the chicken was no longer there.
   d) the chicken was served.

5. Which words from the text are meant by the following definition? Write down the words only.

   a) A ... is a set of instructions for cooking a dish. 1 –
   b) The ... is the part of the stove which is used for roasting and baking. 1 –

Replace only the underlined words without changing the meaning of the sentences.

	C	L
6. They depended on one another for assistance . . . (line 5)	1	–
7. She rushed to the phone . . . (line 15)	1	1
8. They looked at each other in amazement . . . (line 27)	1	1

What are the British equivalents of the following American words?

Example:

American English:	British English:
fire department	fire brigade

		C	L
9. apartment	. . .	1	–
10. elevator	. . .	1	–

Give a definition of the following words as they are used in the text.

	C	L
11. A pioneer (line 4)	2	2
12. An immigrant (line 11)	2	2
13. A fireman (line 20)	2	2

Questions on the text
(Answer in complete sentences.)

	C	L
14. What should Mara have done when she left home?	1	2
15. Why did Mara phone the Fire Department? Give two reasons in one sentence.	2	2
16. Why did Mara's friends think she was going to be disappointed?	2	2
17. Why did Mara's friends accompany her to her apartment?	1	2

Additional questions (Answer each question in about 10–15 words.)

	C	L
18. What are the Fire Department's functions? Name two items.	2	2
19. Would it have been fair to ask Mara to pay the Fire Department's costs? Give a reason for your opinion.	2	2
20. Why do you think the fireman wrote the recipe?	2	2
21. Why do you think Mara forgot to turn off the stove? Give a reason for your answer.	2	2

Complete the following sentences with the equivalents of the German word »sich«.

	C	L
22. Often the colonists couldn't manage alone, they had to help	1	–
23. All the people at the picnic enjoyed	1	–
24. American neighbors visit . . . more often than people in Europe do.	1	–

Complete the following sentences.

	C	L
25. If the fireman hadn't switched off the stove the chicken	–	2
26. This is an example . . . proves that the Americans can be very helpful.	–	1

What did they really say? (Use direct speech.)

	C	L
27. One of Mara's friends remarked that obviously a fireman had been there.	–	2
28. Mara said that she would never forget to turn off the oven again.	–	2
29. Mara tried the salad and said it was abolutely delicious.	–	1

C L

Rewrite the following sentences and fill in the correct forms of the words in brackets.

30. Mara wanted to thank the fireman for . . . (help) her in such a friendly way. – 1
31. When Mara and her friends arrived at the apartment the fireman . . . (leave/already). – 2
32. There are many examples of helpfulness . . . (find) in everyday life. – 1
33. The Americans are also . . . (say/be) fond of loud colors and big cars. – 2

Replace the underlined words by one word or expression of the same meaning.

34. Mara used electricitiy <u>in a</u> very <u>thoughtless way</u>. – 1
35. In future she will use it <u>with greater care</u>. – 2

Rewrite the following sentences replacing the -ing forms by clauses.

36. On coming back she explained what she had done. – 2
37. On the table he had left a note telling her to be more careful next time. – 2
38. Being an immigrant she had unlimited faith in the goodwill of Americans. – 2

What do you think the fireman George Bell wrote as a polite warning? Use the words given below in their correct forms and fill in the missing parts.

(This exercise can be replaced by 40. Translation.)

39. Dear . . .,

    . . . (switch off) . . . (electrical appliances) . . . (leave home). If . . ., . . . (expensive) . . . (dangerous) . . . (you) . . . (neighbors). . . . (careful) . . . (future).

    . . . sincerely,

    . . . – 12

40. **Translate from line 2** (the Americans . . .) to line 6 (. . . stay alive.)
    This exercise can be replaced by 39.) 12 –

Proof? 1979 B

One evening in November, William Howard was having a snack in a cafeteria near Victoria Station. There was a girl sitting opposite him. As she rose to go, her place was taken by a young man, who sighed as he sat down.

»You don't seem very happy,« said Howard. »No, I'm not,« answered the man. »I've just done a very silly thing. I came up to London this afternoon to stay at the White Hart Hotel, and when I got there, I discovered that it had closed down. A taxi driver took me to another hotel, where I was able to book a room. I immediately wrote to my parents, giving them the address of the new hotel, and then I went out to buy some chewing-gum; I'm so used to chewing gum in bed that I simply can't get to sleep without it, you know. It took me some time to find a shop that was still open, and after that I strolled about a bit. After a while I realized that I had forgotten both the name of the hotel and the street it was in. My parents will receive the letter tomorrow, so I shall be able to phone them and ask for the address, but in the meantime, I'm stuck here without any money and with nowhere to go for the night. – You think I've told you an impossible story, don't you?«

»Well, it's not impossible,« said Howard, »but can you show me the chewing-gum?« The young man felt in the pockets of his overcoat and then jumped to his feet. »I must have lost it,« he said and left without another word.

When he had left, Howard noticed a packet of chewing-gum lying under the table. It had evidently fallen out of the youth's overcoat. Howard picked up the chewing-gum and rushed out into the street at once to look for the young man. Finally, he caught sight of him.

»Look!« he said. »The chewing-gum! I found it under the table after you had left. Now I know your story is true. Please excuse me for not believing you. May I lend you some money? You can return it to me at this address.« The youth thanked him and walked on.

When Howard returned to the cafeteria to pay his bill, he saw a young girl looking for something under his table. He recognized her as the girl who had been sitting there before. »Have you lost something?« he asked. »Yes, a packet of chewing-gum.«

Proof? C L

Multiple choice.
Which answer is correct according to the text?
Write down the number and letter only.

1. »I'm stuck here« (line 18) means 1 –
   a) I can't get away from here.
   b) I like this place.
   c) I'm well-known here.
   d) I'm familiar with this area.
   e) I'm trying to hide here.

2. »He strolled about a bit« (line 15) means 1 –
   a) he was looking for something.
   b) he went for a walk.
   c) he tried to find his way.
   d) he didn't know where to go.
   e) he was in a hurry.

3. In the sentence »It had evidently fallen out of the youth's overcoat« (line 26) **evidently** can be replaced by 1 –
   a) unfortunately
   b) finally
   c) unluckily
   d) obviously
   e) suddenly.

Define the following words:

4. snack (line 2) 1 2
5. address (line 11) 2 2
6. overcoat (line 22) 2 2

Finish the following sentences using the opposites of the words underlined. Write down the missing words only, in their correct forms.

	C	L
7. It wasn't easy to find a shop that was still <u>open</u>. Most shops were already	1	1
8. He had <u>forgotten</u> the name of the hotel. He could not . . . the street it was in, either.	1	1
9. May I <u>lend</u> you some money? – No, thank you, I never . . . anything from strangers.	1	1
10. First Howard didn't <u>believe</u> the young man; he . . . the story.	1	1
Replace only the underlined words or phrases without changing the meaning of the sentences.		
11. The young man <u>jumped to his feet</u>.	2	1
12. Howard <u>rushed</u> out <u>at once</u> to look for the young man.	2	1
13. Finally he <u>caught sight of</u> him.	1	1
14. Now I know <u>your story is true</u>.	2	1
15. You can <u>return</u> the money to me at this address.	1	1
Questions on the text. (Answer in complete sentences.)		
16. Why did the young man tell Howard a story which was not true?	1	1
17. Why did Howard ask the young man to show him the chewing-gum?	1	1
18. Why did the youth leave the cafeteria without another word?	2	2
19. Why was Howard later willing to lend the young man some money?	1	2
Additional questions.		
20. Why might the White Hart Hotel have closed down?	2	2
21. What can a tourist do to make sure of getting back to his hotel?	2	2

Defective dialogue.

At the hotel the young man talked to the manager.
Write down what the manager probably asked.

	C	L
22. Manager: » . . .?« Young man: »No, this is my first visit to London.«	1	2
23. Manager: ». . .?« Young man: »From Edinburgh.«	1	2
24. Manager: ». . .?« Young man: »Oh, no, by train. It's less tiring.«	1	1
25. Manager: ». . .?« Young man: »No, not at all. I was alone in my compartment.«	1	2
26. Manager: ». . .?« Young man: »Less than six hours. It was an Inter-City Train.«	1	2
27. Manager: ». . .?« Young man: »Well, I don't know exactly; perhaps you could tell me what is really worth seeing.« Manager: »Certainly. It'll be a pleasure.«	1	2

On arriving home Willam Howard told his wife about his experience. Fill in the correct forms of the words in brackets. (This exercise can be replaced by exercise 41. Translation.)

	C	L
28. While I . . . (sit) in a cafeteria near Victoria Station	–	2
29. a young man . . . (take) a seat at my table. I asked him	–	1
30. why he . . . (be) so unhappy. He . . . (reply) that he	–	2
31. . . . (not/know) what to do. Then he told me what	–	2
32. . . . (happen) to him. When he had finished he wanted	–	1
33. to know whether I . . . (think) his story . . . (sound) possible.	–	2
34. When I asked him to prove that the story . . . (be) true	–	1
35. he . . . (can/not/find) the packet of chewing-gum.	–	1

Rewrite the following sentences replacing the participial constructions.

	C	L
36. There was a girl sitting opposite him.	–	2
37. I immediately wrote to my parents giving them the address of the new hotel.	–	2
38. The young man, used to chewing gum in bed, left the hotel to buy some.	–	2
39. Howard noticed a packet of chewing-gum lying under the table.	–	2
40. After paying his bill he left the cafeteria.	–	2

Translate from line 11 (. . . and then I went out . . .)
to line 16 (. . . the street it was in.)
(This exercise can be replaced by 28. – 35.)

	C	L
41. . . . and then I went out to buy some chewing-gum;	1	–
I'm so used to chewing gum in bed	2	–
that I simply can't get to sleep	1	–
without it, you know.	1	–
It took me some time to find a shop	1	–
that was still open,	1	–
and after that I strolled about a bit.	1	–
After a while I realized	1	–
that I had forgotten	1	–
both the name of the hotel and the street it was in.	2	–